FISCAL YEAR 2011
REPORT TO THE CONGRESS

U.S. Government
Receivables and Debt Collection
Activities of Federal Agencies

Department of the Treasury
June 2012

DEPARTMENT OF THE TREASURY
WASHINGTON, DC

A MESSAGE FROM THE FISCAL ASSISTANT SECRETARY

I am pleased to present the *Fiscal Year 2011 Report to the Congress on U.S. Government Receivables and Debt Collection Activities of Federal Agencies.* This annual report provides important information to the American public on the status and collection of the Federal government's non-tax receivables and delinquent debts.

At the end of Fiscal Year 2011, outstanding non-tax receivables owed to the United States totaled $778 billion, an increase of $152 billion over last year. Most of these receivables represent loans to students, small business owners, homeowners, farmers, and veterans. Other non-tax receivables owed to the United States include fines and penalties, overpayments, and fees.

Most citizens pay their debts on time. However, at the end of Fiscal Year 2011, delinquent non-tax debts owed to the Federal government rose to $131 billion, an increase of $27.4 billion over the prior fiscal year. The timely and efficient collection of delinquent debts helps fund government operations, maintain key programs and reduce the federal deficit. Thus, it is more important than ever to continue to find ways to cost-effectively collect the government's past-due debts, while, at the same time, providing debtors with due process and the opportunity to repay debts in accordance with their financial ability to pay.

The Debt Collection Improvement Act of 1996 centralized administrative delinquent debt collection functions at the Department of the Treasury (Treasury). Since implementation, Treasury's Financial Management Service (FMS) has collected more than $54 billion for Federal and state agencies, including state child support agencies. In Fiscal Year 2011, FMS collected a record $6 billion at a relatively small cost to the Federal government - $52.42 collected for every $1 spent. Despite these successes, we can do more. FMS is working with its agency partners to develop new ideas to optimize and expand its services to increase collections. In times of reduced agency budgets, it is more critical than ever to prioritize and centralize the collection of the Federal government's receivables so that limited resources may be allocated to meet the important needs of our citizens.

Richard L. Gregg

FISCAL YEAR 2011 REPORT TO THE CONGRESS:
U.S. GOVERNMENT RECEIVABLES AND
DEBT COLLECTION ACTIVITIES OF FEDERAL AGENCIES

A Message from the Fiscal Assistant Secretary

I. Overview

The Secretary of the Treasury (Secretary) reports to Congress annually on the Federal government's outstanding non-tax receivables and debt collection activities. As required by Federal law (31 U.S.C. § 3719), this report includes information that Federal agencies provide to the Secretary on the status of their accounts receivable and delinquent debts, as reported on the Treasury Report on Receivables and Debt Collection Activities (TROR). For more information about the TROR, visit *www.fms.treas.gov/debt*.

In furtherance of the policies promulgated by Congress and the President, Federal agencies make loans directly to borrowers, guarantee loans made by private lending institutions, and impose fines and penalties. This activity results in the creation of accounts receivable as assets of the government. In addition, Federal agencies award grants and make payments, which, in certain circumstances, can also result in the creation of accounts receivable.

In Fiscal Year (FY) 2011, the government's outstanding non-tax receivables totaled $778 billion, an increase of $152 billion over FY 2010.

When the government's receivables are not paid by the applicable due date or in the appropriate manner, they become delinquent debts. In FY 2011, delinquent non-tax debts owed to the United States totaled $131 billion, a 27% increase over FY 2010.

Each Federal agency is required to make every reasonable effort to collect its delinquent debts, using collection tools described in this report. In FY 2011, Federal agencies collected $18.3 billion of delinquent debt. The Department of the Treasury (Treasury) and the Department of Justice share responsibility for setting governmentwide policy on delinquent non-tax debt collection, and each plays a major role in the centralized collection of delinquent non-tax debt.

- **Treasury's Financial Management Service (FMS)** collected $6.17 billion in delinquent debt in FY 2011 on behalf of Federal and state agencies, a 13.2% increase over FY 2010. This is the highest amount collected by Treasury in a single fiscal year since it began its governmentwide delinquent debt collection programs in 1996 with the enactment of the Debt Collection Improvement Act (DCIA). Of that amount, $2.72 billion represents Federal non-tax debt collections. Since 1996, Treasury has recovered more than $54 billion on behalf of Federal and state agencies, including $21.5 billion in Federal delinquent non-tax debt, $3.2 billion in Federal delinquent tax debt, and $29.5 billion in delinquent debt owed to state agencies, including $25.9 billion in delinquent child support obligations.

- The **Department of Justice (DOJ)** collected $4.9 billion in FY 2011 on delinquent debts owed to Federal agencies through its civil litigation program. DOJ has collected a total of $18.4 billion through civil litigation in the last five fiscal years.

II. *Receivables Owed to the United States*

A. *Total Receivables*

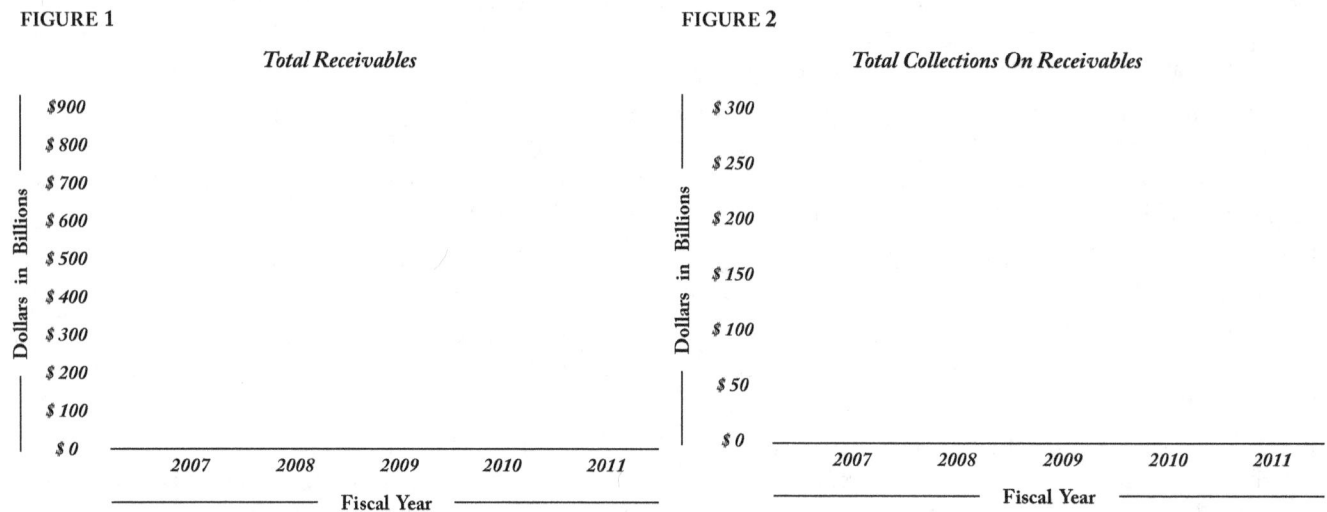

FIGURE 1

Total Receivables

FIGURE 2

Total Collections On Receivables

SOURCE: TREASURY REPORT ON RECEIVABLES AND DEBT COLLECTION ACTIVITIES — FOURTH QUARTER FY 2011

At the end of FY 2011, non-tax receivables owed to the United States totaled $777.8 billion, an increase of $152 billion from FY 2010. Collections on governmentwide receivables in FY 2011 totaled $245.3 billion, an increase of $22.4 billion from FY 2010.

The Departments of Education (Education) and Agriculture (USDA) held the largest portfolios, which totaled $621 billion and represented 80% of the government's total receivables.

- **Education:** At the end of FY 2011, Education's outstanding receivables totaled $504.7 billion, 65% of the government's total receivables. Federal Direct Student Loans ($355.6 billion) and Defaulted Guaranteed Student Loans ($44.4 billion) accounted for the majority of the receivables. In FY 2011, Education collected $56.2 billion, an increase of $3.4 billion over FY 2010, including loan consolidations.

- **USDA:** At the end of FY 2011, USDA's outstanding receivables totaled $116.2 billion, 15% of the government's total receivables. Five program areas of the USDA accounted for over $109 billion of its receivables: Rural Electric & Telephone Revolving Fund ($45.7 billion), Rural Housing Insurance Fund ($27.7 billion), Rural Development Insurance Fund ($16.1 billion), Commodity Credit Corporation ($11.8 billion) and Farm Service Agency ($8.4 billion). FY 2011 receivables collections totaled $24.1 billion.

B. Direct and Guaranteed Loans

At the end of FY 2011, Federal loan programs (direct and defaulted guaranteed) totaled $693.7 billion, or 89.2% of total receivables. At the end of FY 2010, loan programs represented 87.3% of total receivables.

C. Non-Loan Receivables (Administrative Debt)

Non-loan receivables, or administrative debt, account for the remainder of the receivables. Non-loan receivables include fines, penalties, and overpayments. At the end of FY 2011, non-loan receivables totaled $84.1 billion, or 10.8% of total receivables, down from 12.8% of total receivables in FY 2010.

D. Interest, Penalties and Costs

Generally, agencies are required to add interest, penalties and administrative costs to receivables owed to the United States in accordance with applicable loan documents and statutory requirements. <u>See</u>, <u>e.g.</u> 31 U.S.C. §3717. Of the $777.8 billion in receivables at the end of FY 2011, $32.7 billion represents unpaid interest, penalties and administrative costs.

FIGURE 3

Government Loan and Non-Loan Receivables

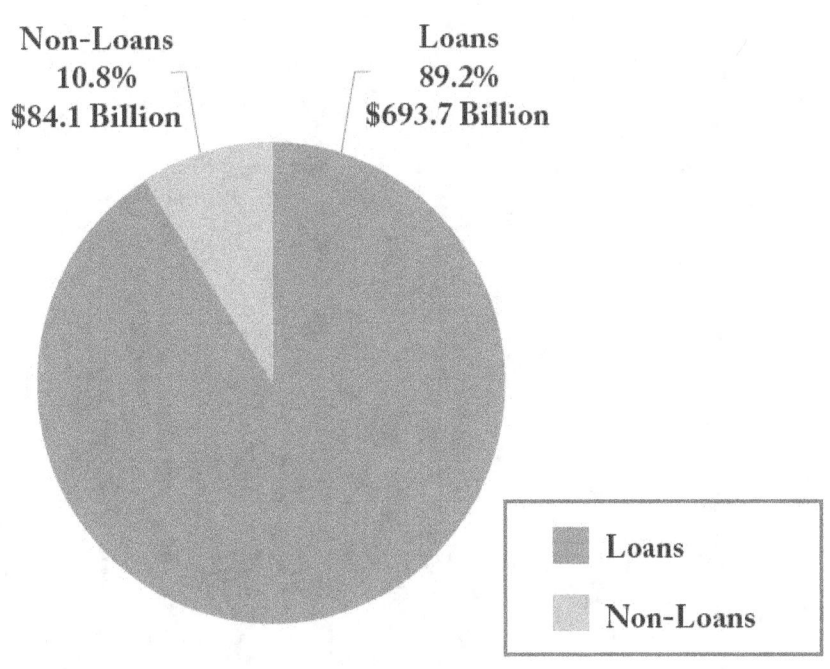

Non-Loans
10.8%
$84.1 Billion

Loans
89.2%
$693.7 Billion

Loans

Non-Loans

SOURCE: TREASURY REPORT ON RECEIVABLES AND DEBT
COLLECTION ACTIVITIES — FOURTH QUARTER FY 2011

III. *Delinquent Non-Tax Debts Owed to the United States*

Along with the increase in receivables, delinquencies at the end of FY 2011 rose to $131 billion, an increase of $27.4 billion, or 27%, from the previous year.

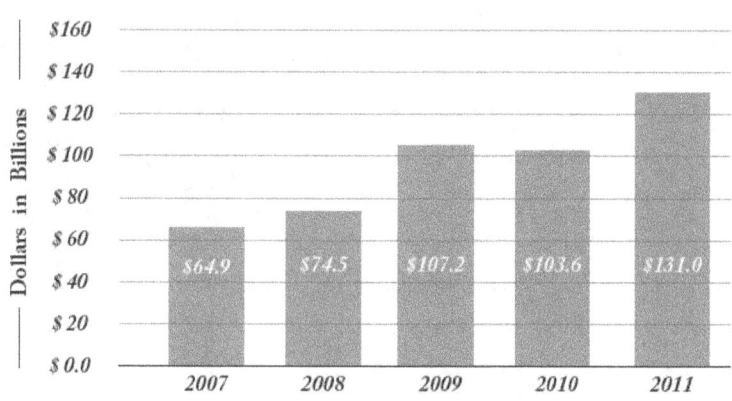

FIGURE 4

Governmentwide Delinquencies

SOURCE: TREASURY REPORT ON RECEIVABLES AND DEBT
COLLECTION ACTIVITIES — FOURTH QUARTER FY 2011

FIGURE 5

A. By Age

The majority of delinquent non-tax debts owed to the Federal government at the end of FY 2011, $87.5 billion of the total portfolio, were less than two years delinquent. Debts delinquent more than six years totaled $17.1 billion.

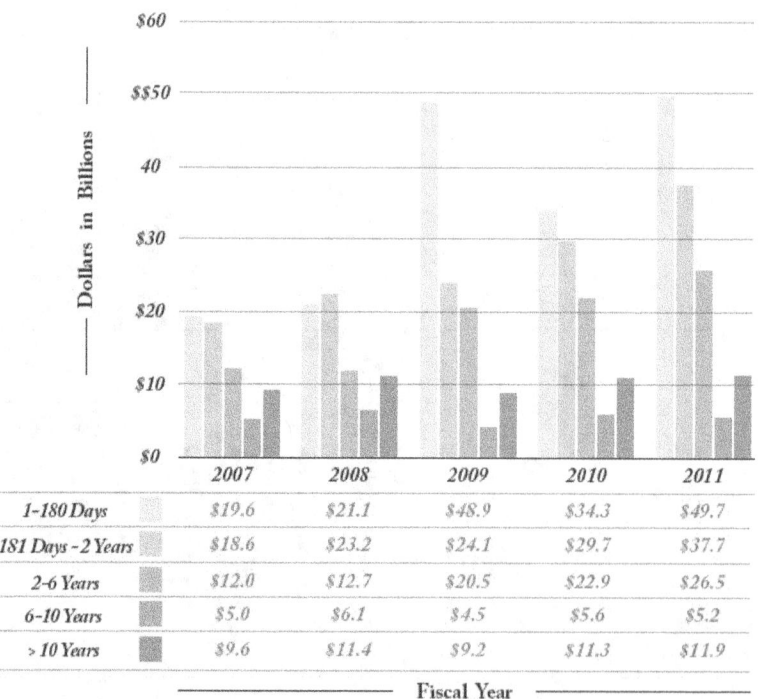

Aging of Governmentwide Delinquencies

	2007	2008	2009	2010	2011
1-180 Days	$19.6	$21.1	$48.9	$34.3	$49.7
181 Days - 2 Years	$18.6	$23.2	$24.1	$29.7	$37.7
2-6 Years	$12.0	$12.7	$20.5	$22.9	$26.5
6-10 Years	$5.0	$6.1	$4.5	$5.6	$5.2
> 10 Years	$9.6	$11.4	$9.2	$11.3	$11.9

Fiscal Year

SOURCE: TREASURY REPORT ON RECEIVABLES AND DEBT
COLLECTION ACTIVITIES — FOURTH QUARTER FY 2011

B. By Agency

At the end of FY 2011, $114.2 billion (87%) of the government's delinquent debts were owed to five agencies: Education, Small Business Administration (SBA), Department of Housing & Urban Development (HUD), Department of Defense (DOD), and Social Security Administration (SSA), as shown in the accompanying table and its related chart.

FIGURE 6

Delinquencies : Top Five Agencies
(in billions)

Agency	FY 2011	% Change from FY 2010
Education	$92.1	+ 29%
SBA	$6.6	+ 12%
HUD	$5.6	+ 224% *
DOD	$5.3	+ 2%
SSA	$4.7	+ 12%
Total of Above	$114.2	+ 29%
Total Government	$131.0	+ 27%

SOURCE: TREASURY REPORT ON RECEIVABLES AND DEBT COLLECTION ACTIVITIES — FOURTH QUARTER FY 2011

FIGURE 7

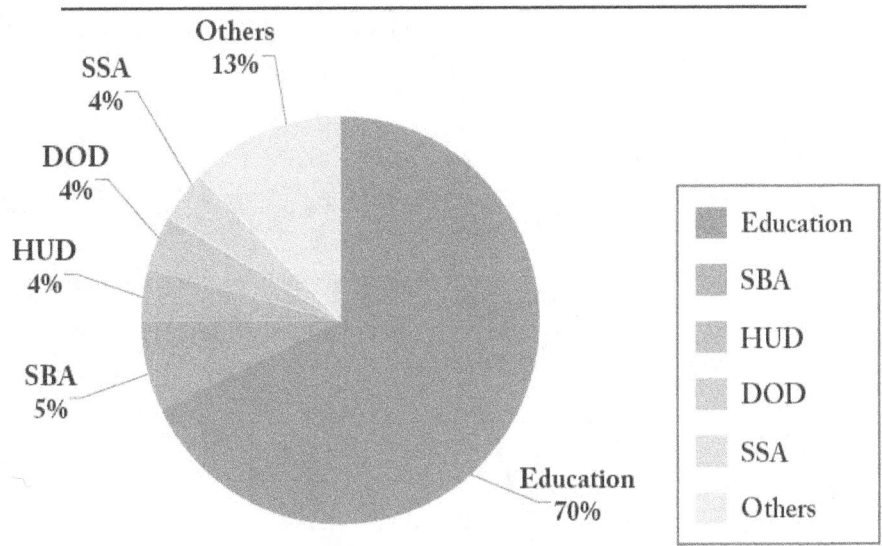

Delinquencies : Top Five Agencies

SOURCE: TREASURY REPORT ON RECEIVABLES AND DEBT COLLECTION ACTIVITIES — FOURTH QUARTER FY 2011

* The significant increase in HUD's delinquent debt portfolio was driven primarily by large volume defaults under the Government National Mortgage Association (GNMA) loan program and HUD's housing loan programs (Elderly and Handicapped, Title I, Single Family, and Multi-Family).

C. By Debt Type

At the end of FY 2011, Federal loan program delinquencies comprised 82% of total delinquencies, down slightly from 83% at the end of FY 2010.

FIGURE 8

Distribution of Receivables and Delinquencies as of 9/30/11

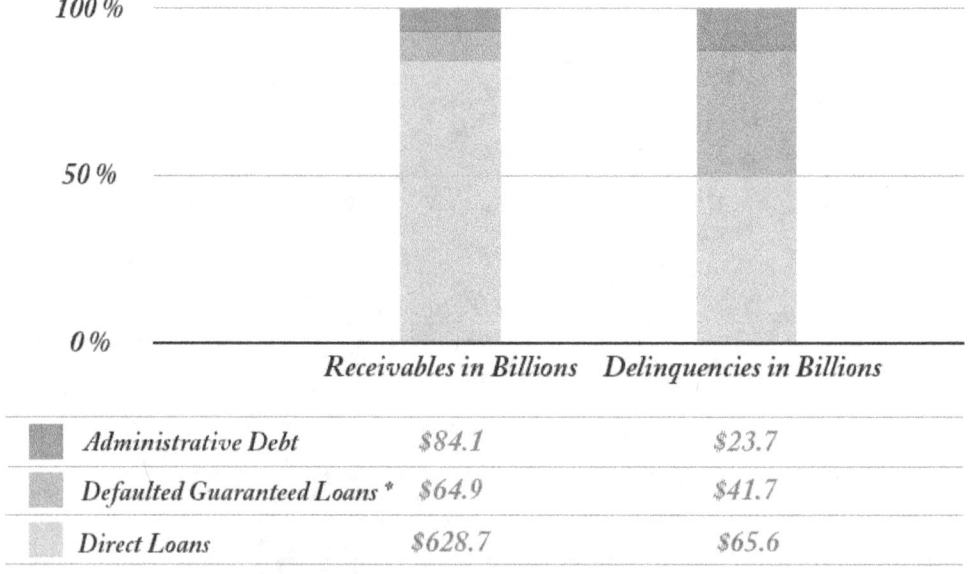

	Receivables in Billions	Delinquencies in Billions
Administrative Debt	$84.1	$23.7
Defaulted Guaranteed Loans *	$64.9	$41.7
Direct Loans	$628.7	$65.6

* Receivables amount includes rehabilitated loans

SOURCE: TREASURY REPORT ON RECEIVABLES AND DEBT COLLECTION ACTIVITIES —
FOURTH QUARTER FY 2011

IV. Delinquent Debt Collection Activities

In FY 2011, Federal agencies collected $18.3 billion of delinquent non-tax debt using a variety of tools. Collection tools include offset, administrative wage garnishment, litigation, asset sales, and utilization of private collection agencies. In addition, Federal agencies are generally required to refer their debts to Treasury for collection as soon as the debts become 180 days delinquent.

A. Administrative Wage Garnishment (AWG) Collections

Federal agencies are authorized to garnish a delinquent debtor's non-Federal wages without obtaining a court order (See, 31 U.S.C. § 3720D). This process is known as "administrative wage garnishment." Private collection agencies may assist Treasury and other agencies in the initiation of an administrative wage garnishment. The goal of AWG is to ensure that every employed debtor is repaying his or her debts owed to the United States. Before issuing an AWG order, agencies must first provide a debtor with notice and an opportunity to enter into a repayment agreement, dispute the debt, or object to the intended garnishment action. In FY 2011, Federal agencies collected $295.9 million through the use of AWG. Of that total, Treasury collected $27.2 million on behalf of the Federal agencies participating in the Cross-Servicing Program.

B. Private Collection Agency (PCA) Referrals and Collections

Federal agencies are authorized to contract with PCAs to collect delinquent non-tax debts owed to the United States (See, 31 U.S.C. § 3718). PCAs assist Federal agencies in many ways, including by establishing repayment agreements and resolving debts administratively when a debtor is deceased, unable to pay, disabled, bankrupt, or out of business.

- **Treasury** contracts with PCAs to collect delinquent non-tax debts referred by Federal agencies participating in Treasury's Cross-Servicing Program. In FY 2011, Treasury's PCAs collected $93 million, an increase of 3% over FY 2010. Referrals totaled $7.9 billion.

- **Education** contracts with PCAs to assist in collecting defaulted student loan debts. In FY 2011, Education's PCAs collected $2.6 billion, an increase of 12% over FY 2010. Referrals totaled $31.35 billion.

- **HHS's Program Support Center (PSC)** contracts with a PCA to collect delinquent debts. PSC's PCA referrals and collections increased in FY 2011 due to health profession guaranteed loan referrals and referrals of delinquent repatriation debts arising from the evacuation of U.S. citizens from Haiti following the earthquake in January 2010.

1. Referrals to PCAs

FIGURE 9

Referrals to PCAs
(in millions)

HHS	*$69*	*$35*	*$51*	*$17*	*$46*
Treasury	*$3,341*	*$4,454*	*$6,379*	*$6,984*	*$7,904*
Education	*$18,982*	*$23,863*	*$24,470*	*$28,845*	*$31,350*

SOURCES: DEPARTMENT OF HEALTH AND HUMAN SERVICES, PROGRAM SUPPORT CENTER
DEPARTMENT OF THE TREASURY, FINANCIAL MANAGEMENT SERVICE
DEPARTMENT OF EDUCATION, DEFAULT RESOLUTION GROUP

2. Collections by PCAs

FIGURE 10

Total Collections by PCAs
(in millions)

HHS	*$7.4*	*$3.8*	*$2.2*	*$1.7*	*$2.9*
Treasury[1]	*$74.6*	*$82.8*	*$132.1*	*$90.3*	*$93.0*
Education[1,2]	*$2,046.0*	*$2,291.0*	*$2,416.0*	*$2,354.0*	*$2,644.0*

[1] Includes collections by administrative wage garnishment from employed debtors

[2] Includes loan consolidations and rehabilitations

SOURCES: DEPARTMENT OF HEALTH AND HUMAN SERVICES, PROGRAM SUPPORT CENTER
DEPARTMENT OF THE TREASURY, FINANCIAL MANAGEMENT SERVICE
DEPARTMENT OF EDUCATION, DEFAULT RESOLUTION GROUP

C. Department of the Treasury's Debt Collection Programs

Generally, Federal agencies are required to refer non-tax debts more than 180 days delinquent to Treasury for collection through its Treasury Offset Program (TOP) and its Cross-Servicing Program. For debts submitted to TOP, Treasury intercepts eligible Federal and state payments and applies them to a payee's delinquent debts. For debts submitted to its Cross-Servicing Program, Treasury contacts debtors by demand letters and telephone calls, negotiates payment agreements, submits debts to TOP, refers debts to private collection agencies and the Department of Justice, reports debts to credit bureaus, and initiates administrative wage garnishment. Before submitting a debt to Treasury, agencies must send the debtor a notice describing the debt, the collection actions to be taken, and the opportunities available to the debtor to repay or challenge the debt.

Certain types of debts are ineligible for referral to TOP or Cross-Servicing, including debts owed by foreign sovereigns, debts that are the subject of an appeal, forbearance agreement, litigation, foreclosure, or bankruptcy. Certain other debts are eligible for TOP and Cross-Servicing, but are exempt from the general mandatory requirement that they be referred to Cross-Servicing, including debts being serviced by a PCA, debts being collected by internal offset or administrative wage garnishment, and Treasury-exempted debts.

At the end of FY 2011, of the $112.9 billion in non-tax debts more than 180 days delinquent, $68.6 billion were required to be submitted to TOP, an increase of $8.4 billion from the end of FY 2010. Delinquent debts totaling $20.4 billion were required to be submitted to Treasury's Cross-Servicing Program, an increase of $2.8 billion over FY 2010. Of the $112.9 billion, $31.7 billion have been written off for accounting purposes, but are still eligible for collection.

FIGURE 11

Debts Required to be Referred to Treasury

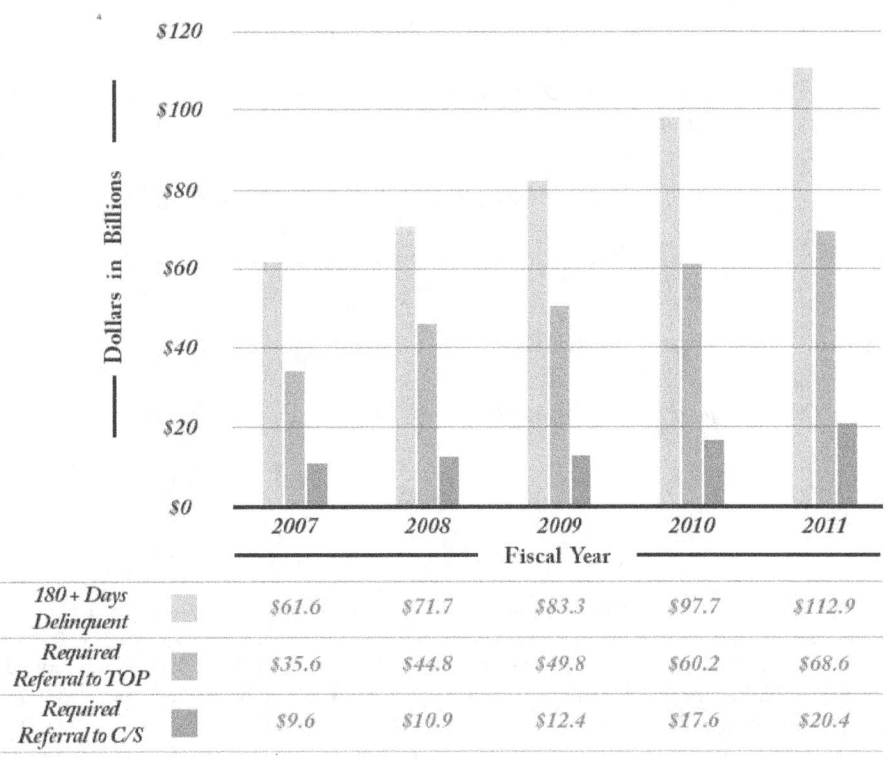

	2007	2008	2009	2010	2011
180 + Days Delinquent	$61.6	$71.7	$83.3	$97.7	$112.9
Required Referral to TOP	$35.6	$44.8	$49.8	$60.2	$68.6
Required Referral to C/S	$9.6	$10.9	$12.4	$17.6	$20.4

SOURCE: TREASURY REPORT ON RECEIVABLES AND DEBT COLLECTION ACTIVITIES
— FOURTH QUARTER FY 2011

1. Referrals to TOP

In FY 2011, $112.5 billion in Federal non-tax debts were submitted to TOP, a 19% increase over FY 2010.[1]

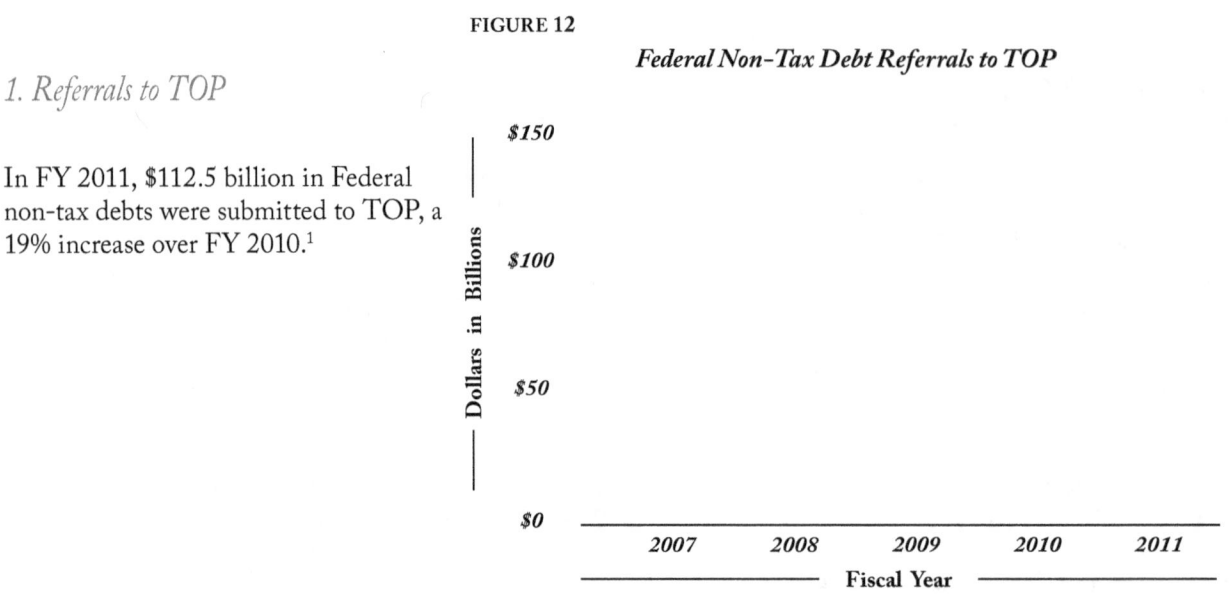

FIGURE 12

Federal Non-Tax Debt Referrals to TOP

SOURCE: DEPARTMENT OF THE TREASURY, FINANCIAL MANAGEMENT SERVICE

2. TOP Collections

In FY 2011, Treasury collected, through TOP, $2.6 billion in non-tax debts owed to Federal agencies.[2]

TOP-eligible payments include Federal tax refunds, Social Security, retirement, salary, vendor, and other Federal payments, as well as state tax refunds and other payments made by several states participating in TOP.

FIGURE 13

TOP Collections of Federal Non-tax Debt by Payment Type
(in millions)

Federal Tax Refund	$1,195.0	$1,948.0	$1,400.0	$1,852.0	$2,180.0
Federal Nontax Payments	$182.6	$216.2	$511.9	$313.0	$390.0
State Payments	N/A	$5.5	$12.2	$12.4	$7.4

SOURCE: DEPARTMENT OF THE TREASURY, FINANCIAL MANAGEMENT SERVICE

[1] In addition to collecting Federal non-tax debt, TOP is used to collect delinquent Federal taxes and state debts, including delinquent child support obligations. In FY 2011, $211.3 billion in Federal tax debts and $132.4 billion in state debts were referred to TOP. See Appendix IV for more information.

[2] In addition, Treasury collects delinquent Federal taxes and debts owed to state agencies, including delinquent child support obligations, through TOP. In FY 2011, Treasury collected $614 million in delinquent Federal tax debt and $2.8 billion for state agencies, including $2.3 billion in delinquent child support in all 50 states and the District of Columbia. Treasury collects child support obligations in collaboration with the Department of Health and Human Services' Office of Child Support Enforcement. Treasury collects delinquent state income tax obligations for 40 states and the District of Columbia. In February 2011, Treasury began collecting unemployment compensation debts for states through TOP. See Appendix IV for more information.

3. Referrals to the Cross-Servicing Program

As of September 30, 2011, the active Federal delinquent debt inventory in the Cross-Servicing Program was $19.1 billion, an 8% increase from the prior fiscal year. In FY 2011, Federal agencies referred a total of $3.6 billion to the program.

FIGURE 14

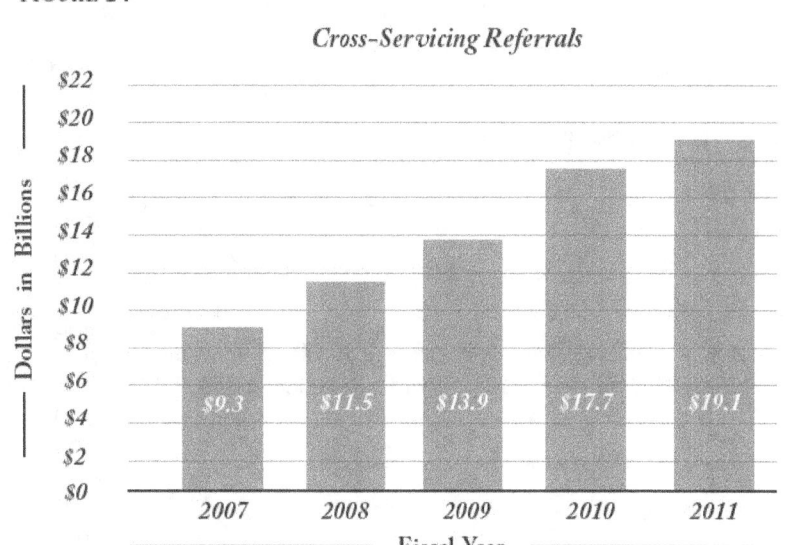

Cross-Servicing Referrals

SOURCE: DEPARTMENT OF THE TREASURY, FINANCIAL MANAGEMENT SERVICE

4. Cross-Servicing Collections

In FY 2011, Treasury collected $231 million through its Cross-Servicing Program. Of that amount, $45.3 million was recovered by employees of Debt Management Services (DMS), an area within Treasury's FMS, $93 million was collected by Treasury's PCAs, and $93.2 million was collected through TOP.

FIGURE 15

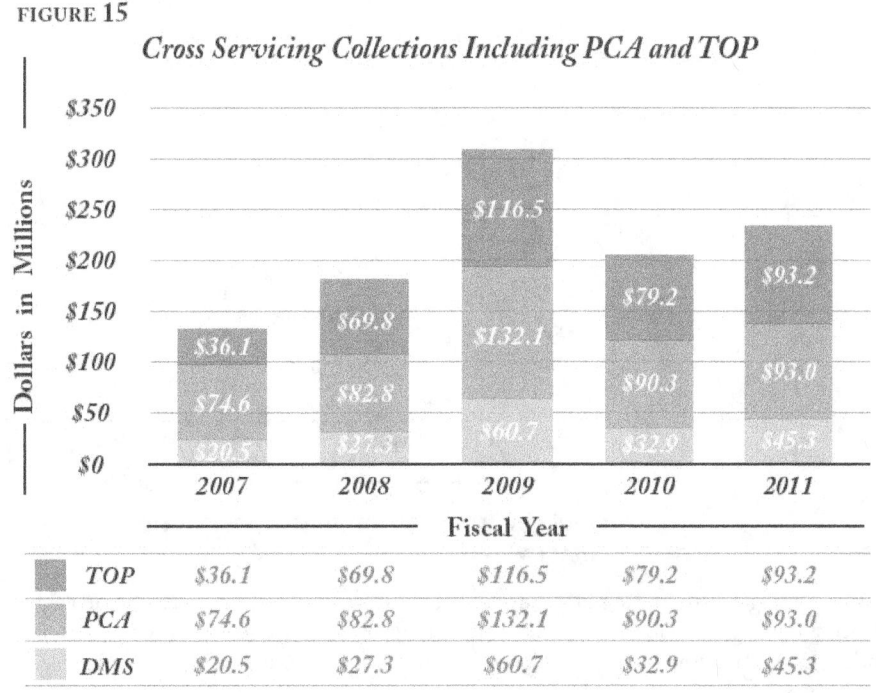

Cross Servicing Collections Including PCA and TOP

	2007	2008	2009	2010	2011
TOP	$36.1	$69.8	$116.5	$79.2	$93.2
PCA	$74.6	$82.8	$132.1	$90.3	$93.0
DMS	$20.5	$27.3	$60.7	$32.9	$45.3

SOURCE: DEPARTMENT OF THE TREASURY, FINANCIAL MANAGEMENT SERVICE

D. Enforced Debt Collection by the Department of Justice (DOJ)

When a Federal agency cannot collect a debt administratively, the agency may refer the debt to DOJ to pursue enforced collection through the courts.[3]

1. Referrals to DOJ

In FY 2011, Federal agencies referred 16,000 cases totaling $6.1 billion to DOJ for enforced collection.

2. Collections by DOJ

In FY 2011, DOJ collected $4.9 billion for Federal agencies through enforced collection.

FIGURE **16**

Referrals to DOJ

2007	9,718	$5.0
2008	11,559	$3.8
2009	11,088	$5.2
2010	11,531	$7.6
2011	16,487	$6.1

SOURCE: DEPARTMENT OF JUSTICE, OFFICE OF DEBT COLLECTION MANAGEMENT

FIGURE **17**

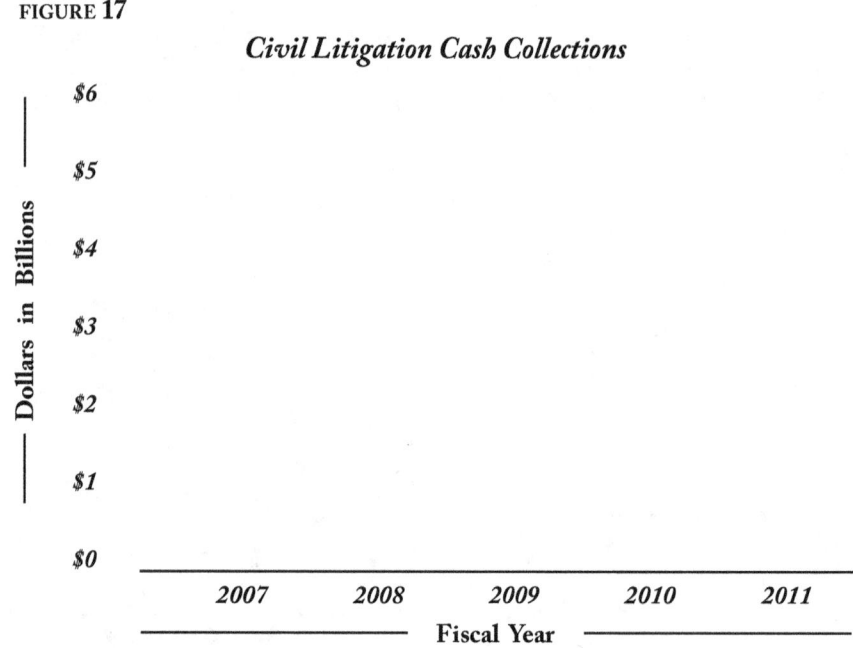

Civil Litigation Cash Collections

SOURCE: DEPARTMENT OF JUSTICE, OFFICE OF DEBT COLLECTION MANAGEMENT

[3] DOJ is responsible for instituting and defending litigation on behalf of most Federal agencies. Some agencies have independent litigation authority, which allows agencies to institute and defend their own cases in court. Information on judicial collections from agencies with independent litigation authority is included in this report as part of total DOJ collections.

E. Department of Education Student Loans

The Department of Education collects delinquent student loans directly and through a network of Guaranty Agencies (GAs). Education's Default Resolution Group (DRG) services Education's defaulted student loans (loans delinquent more than 270 days) and a small number of student grant overpayments. DRG uses a variety of debt collection tools, including private collection agencies, administrative wage garnishment, and offset. The GAs manage current loans and collect defaulted loans using the same tools as DRG. Education works with the GAs to ensure that all eligible debts are certified to TOP in order to maximize the potential for collection.

FIGURE **18**

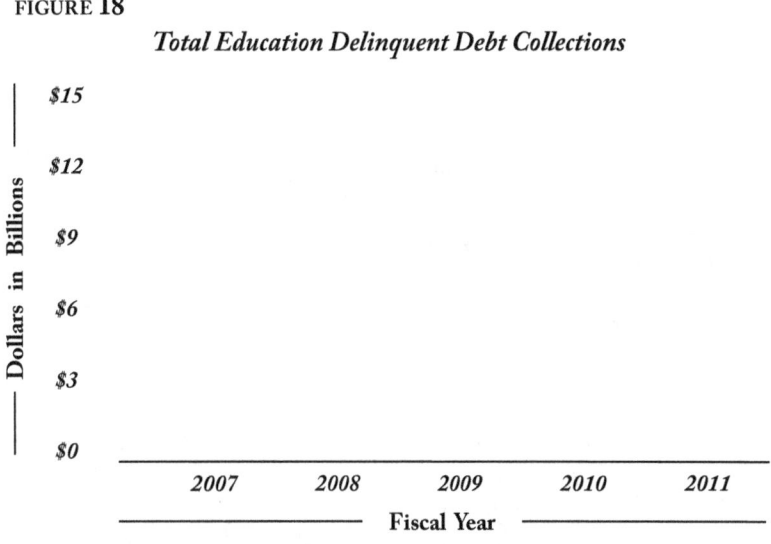

Total Education Delinquent Debt Collections

SOURCE: DEPARTMENT OF EDUCATION, DEFAULT RESOLUTION GROUP

FIGURE **19**

Education Collections by Debt Collection Tool – 5 Year Comparison
(in millions)

Private Collection Agency (PCA): Regular Collections	$368	$376	$318	$300	$362
PCA: Administrative Wage Garnishment (AWG)	$271	$296	$317	$339	$349
PCA: Loan Consolidations	$155	$212	$367	$367	$476
PCA: Loan Rehabilitations	$1,252	$1,406	$1,348	$1,347	$1,457
Dept of Justice: Litigation	$13	$11	$9	$9	$10
DRG: Internal Offset	$.1	$.1	$.1	$.1	$.5
DRG/GAs: AWG	$435	$522	$607	$621	$662
DRG/GAs: Treasury Offset Program	$844	$1,374	$1,120	$1,408	$1,651
DRG/GAs: Regular Collections	$643	$704	$718	$736	$785
DRG/GAs: Loan Consolidations	$1,168	$1,360	$1,930	$2,039	$2,545
DRG/GAs: Total Loan Rehabilitations	$1,771	$2,315	$2,018	$3,127	$3,707

Notes:

1. PCA data is for the DRG portfolio only. Education does not require the GAs to report the portion of their collections attributed to their PCAs.

2. PCAs are authorized to use AWG on Education's behalf.

3. Loan rehabilitation occurs when a debtor makes at least nine (9) full payments of an agreed amount within 10 months, and is the preferred collection method when a borrower is unable to make a one-time payment in full.

4. "DRG Internal Offset" represents collections through Education's non-centralized Federal Employee Salary Offset Program. While DRG now participates in the centralized TOP, which includes the offset of Federal salary payments, the former program is still receiving payments. DRG has recovered approximately $3 million dollars from Federal salaries through TOP's centralized process since the inception of the program in FY 2010.

SOURCE: DEPARTMENT OF EDUCATION, DEFAULT RESOLUTION GROUP

F. Department of Health and Human Services Program Support Center

In 1995, the U.S. Department of Health and Human Services (HHS) established the Program Support Center (PSC), Debt Collection Center. The PSC is a Treasury-designated debt collection center that collects debts on a fee-for-service basis for 11 different agencies within HHS and several agencies outside of HHS. In addition, the PSC serves as the HHS conduit for referrals to Treasury for both TOP and Cross-Servicing. Collections since inception of the PSC debt collection program have exceeded $5 billion.

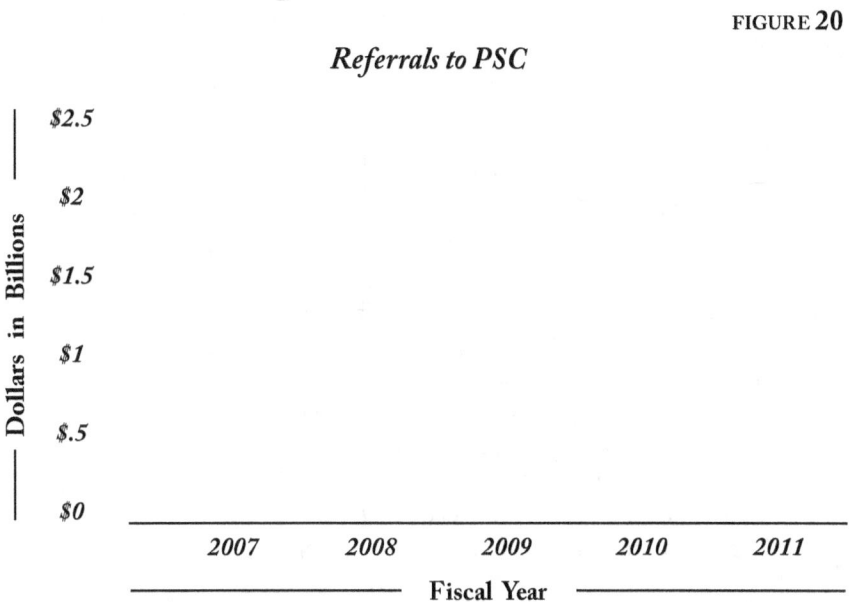

FIGURE 20

Referrals to PSC

SOURCE: DEPARTMENT OF HEALTH AND HUMAN SERVICES, PROGRAM SUPPORT CENTER

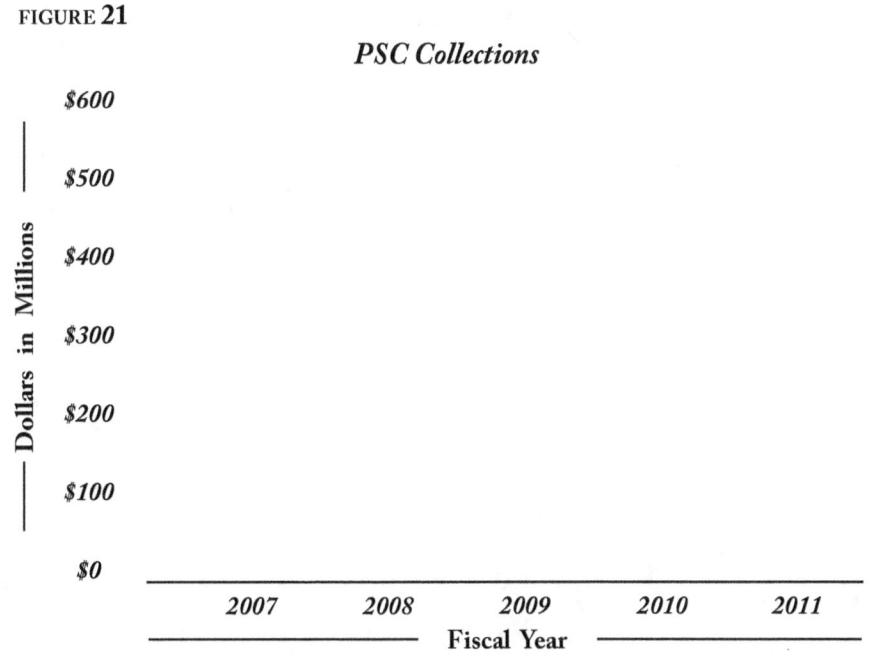

FIGURE 21

PSC Collections

SOURCE: DEPARTMENT OF HEALTH AND HUMAN SERVICES, PROGRAM SUPPORT CENTER

V. *Write-Offs Of Delinquent Debts*

Agencies are generally required to "write-off" debts that are two years delinquent (See Office of Management and Budget Circular A-129). By writing off their uncollectible debts, agencies more accurately reflect the value of their receivables on the books of the United States.

In FY 2011, write-offs totaled $13.8 billion, an increase from FY 2010 of $2.4 billion, or 21%. The agencies with the largest write-off amounts in FY 2011 include the Department of Education ($4.1 billion), Small Business Administration ($2.5 billion) and Social Security Administration ($1 billion).

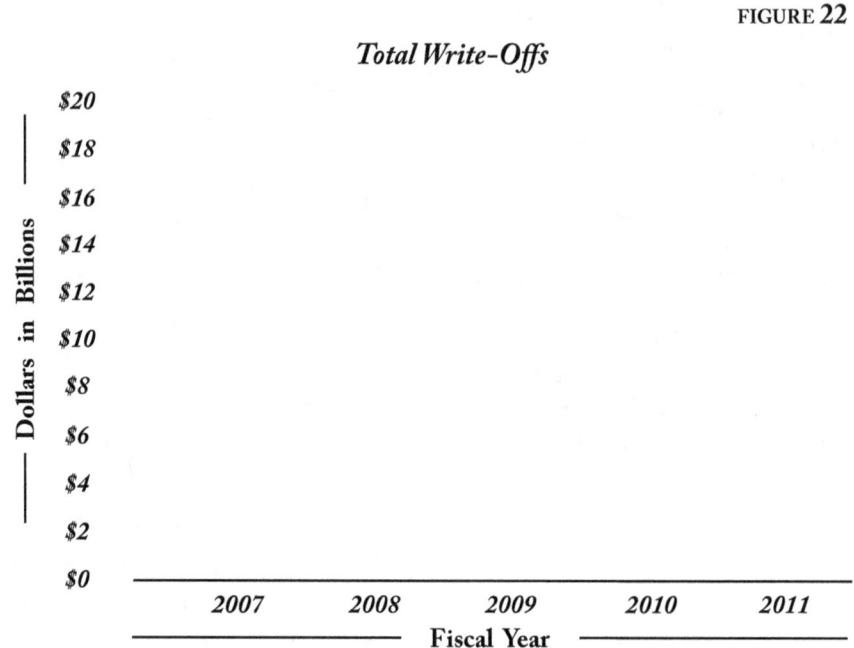

FIGURE 22

Total Write-Offs

SOURCE: TREASURY REPORT ON RECEIVABLES AND DEBT COLLECTION
ACTIVITIES — FOURTH QUARTER FY 2011

Appendix I: Total Federal Receivables and Collections by Agency

At the end of FY 2011, 95% of Federal receivables arose from programs managed by the 10 agencies listed below. The remaining 5% of Federal receivables arose from all other programs.

Total Federal Receivables and Collections by Agency
(in millions)

Education	$504,697	$56,157
USDA	$116,152	$24,050
Treasury	$21,621	$13,936
HUD	$19,047	$9,758
SBA	$16,644	$2,156
SSA	$15,855	$3,633
HHS	$14,515	$39,412
DOD	$11,576	$9,354
Energy	$10,978	$9,725
Export-Import Bank	$9,918	$1,130
Top 10 Total	**$741,001**	**$169,310**
All Other	$36,761	$69,805

SOURCE: TREASURY REPORT ON RECEIVABLES AND DEBT COLLECTION ACTIVITIES — FOURTH QUARTER **FY 2011**

Appendix II: Total Federal Delinquent Debts and Collections by Agency

At the end of FY 2011, 96% of Federal delinquent debt arose from programs managed by the 10 agencies listed below. The remaining 4% of Federal delinquent debt arose from all other programs.

Total Federal Delinquent Debts and Collections by Agency
(in millions)

Education	$92,045	$7,419
SBA	$6,594	$459
HUD	$5,585	$2,971
DOD	$5,292	$1,959
SSA	$4,664	$134
USDA	$4,249	$1,043
HHS	$1,974	$1,175
EPA	$1,899	$546
Export-Import Bank	$1,695	$182
Funds Appropriated to the President	$1,632	$966
Top 10 Total	$125,630	$16,854
All Other	$5,369	$1,419

SOURCE: TREASURY REPORT ON RECEIVABLES AND DEBT COLLECTION ACTIVITIES — FOURTH QUARTER FY 2011

Appendix III: Total Federal Write-Offs by Agency

In FY 2011, 90% of Federal debt write-offs arose from programs managed by the 10 agencies listed below. The remaining 10% of Federal debt write-offs arose from all other programs.

Total Federal Write-Offs By Agency
(in millions)

Education	*$4,086*
SBA	*$2,464*
SSA	*$1,018*
Export–Import Bank	*$960*
HHS	*$934*
VA	*$869*
DHS	*$769*
FTC	*$613*
DOD	*$487*
HUD	*$237*
Top 10 Total	*$12,436*
All Other	*$1,342*

SOURCE: TREASURY REPORT ON RECEIVABLES AND DEBT COLLECTION
ACTIVITIES — FOURTH QUARTER **FY 2011**

Appendix IV: Treasury Offset Program (TOP) Referrals and Collections Including Debts Owed to the Internal Revenue Service and State Agencies

Treasury Offset Program

The Treasury Offset Program (TOP) is the centralized process through which Treasury and other disbursing agencies reduce, or "offset" eligible Federal and state payments, including tax refund payments, to a debtor to satisfy the debtor's past-due Federal non-tax debt and debts owed to state agencies, including child support and unemployment insurance obligations. In addition, the Federal Payment Levy Program, processed through TOP, allows the Internal Revenue Service (IRS) to continuously levy Federal payments due to delinquent Federal taxpayers.

TOP highlights include:

- In FY 2011, more than $6 billion was collected through TOP for Federal and state agencies.

- Child support obligations are submitted to TOP by states through the Department of Health & Human Services, Office of Child Support Enforcement.

- As of September 30, 2011, forty (40) states and the District of Columbia were participating in TOP's state income tax program, whereby Federal tax refunds are offset to collect delinquent state income tax obligations.[4]

- Four states participate in TOP's State Reciprocal Program whereby eligible Federal payments are intercepted to collect debts owed to states, and states intercept state payments to collect delinquent non-tax Federal debts. At least two additional states are expected to join the program in FY 2012, and several others have expressed interest.

- At the end of FY 2011, Federal tax refunds were being offset to collect unemployment compensation debts owed to three states since the program began in February 2011. Other states continue to join the program.

- Through the tax levy program, $614 million of unpaid Federal taxes were collected by TOP.

---

[4] Nine (9) states do not have an income tax.

Referrals to TOP

The amount of Federal and state debt in TOP totaled $456.2 billion as of September 30, 2011.

FIGURE 23

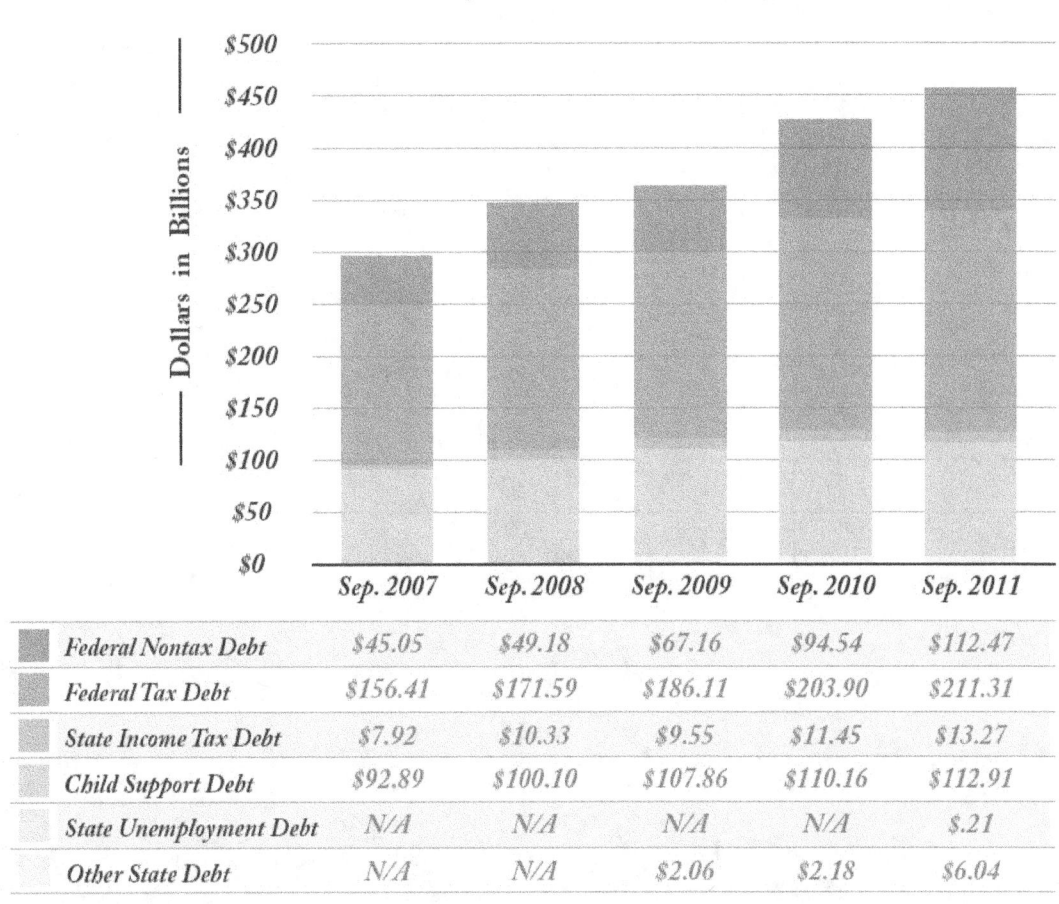

Debt Referrals to the Treasury Offset Program

	Sep. 2007	Sep. 2008	Sep. 2009	Sep. 2010	Sep. 2011
Federal Nontax Debt	$45.05	$49.18	$67.16	$94.54	$112.47
Federal Tax Debt	$156.41	$171.59	$186.11	$203.90	$211.31
State Income Tax Debt	$7.92	$10.33	$9.55	$11.45	$13.27
Child Support Debt	$92.89	$100.10	$107.86	$110.16	$112.91
State Unemployment Debt	N/A	N/A	N/A	N/A	$.21
Other State Debt	N/A	N/A	$2.06	$2.18	$6.04

SOURCE: DEPARTMENT OF THE TREASURY, FINANCIAL MANAGEMENT SERVICE

Collections by TOP

TOP Collections
(in millions)

	Type of Debt	Type of Payment Offset	FY 2007	FY 2008	FY 2009	FY 2010	FY 2011
Federal Debt	Federal Non-tax Debt	Tax Refund Offset	$1,195.0	$1,948.0	$1,400.0	$1,852.0	$2,180.0
	Federal Non-tax Debt	Administrative Offset (Federal + State Payments)	$182.6	$221.7	$524.0	$312.8	$390.4 *
	Federal Tax Debt	Tax Levy (Federal Payments)	$343.0	$400	$497.0	$617.9	$614.3
Total Federal			$1,720.6	$2,569.7	$2,421.0	$2,782.7	$3,184.7
State Debt	Child Support	Tax Refund Offset	$1,696.0	$2,830.0	$2,066.0	$2,086.0	$2,302.0
	State Income Tax Debt	Tax Refund Offset	$219.0	$358.0	$368.0	$435.1	$475.0
	State Unemployment Compensation Debt	Tax Refund Offset	N/A	N/A	N/A	N/A	$25.9
	Child Support	Administrative Offset	$4.2	$4.6	$5.0	$8.3	$10.4
	State Income Tax Debt (Reciprocal Program)	Administrative Offset	N/A	$19.6	$13.0	$9.1	$7.4
	Other State Debt (Reciprocal Program)	Administrative Offset	N/A	$18.6	$12.0	$7.4	$28.8
Total State			$1,919.2	$3,230.8	$2,464.0	$2,545.9	$2,849.5
Total Collected			$3,640	$5,801	$4,885	$5,329	$6,034

*FY 2011 "Administrative Offset — Federal Non-tax Debt" includes collections in the amount of $7.4 million of Federal non-tax debt by states under the Federal-State Reciprocal Offset Program.

SOURCE: DEPARTMENT OF THE TREASURY, FINANCIAL MANAGEMENT SERVICE

Appendix V: Sources of Data

Data contained in this report were obtained from the following sources:

Treasury Report on Receivables and Debt Collection Activities — Fourth Quarter 2011, as reported by Federal agencies to the Department of the Treasury.

Part II - Receivables Owed to the United States

Part III - Delinquent Non-Tax Debts Owed to the United States

Part V - Write-Offs of Delinquent Debts

Appendix I-III

Department of the Treasury, Financial Management Service

Part IV - Delinquent Debt Collection Activities

Appendix IV

Department of Education, Default Resolution Group

Part IV - Delinquent Debt Collection Activities

Department of Health and Human Services, Program Support Center

Part IV - Delinquent Debt Collection Activities

Department of Justice, Office of Debt Collection Management

Part IV - Delinquent Debt Collection Activities